D1584222

This celebration of creativity has been produced and first published in Great Britain in 2006 by:

HMP High Down
High Down Lane
Sutton
Surrey
SM2 5PJ

A catalogue record for this book is available from the British Library

ISBN 10: 0 9552308 0 2

Edited by Douglas Nicolson

I am delighted to see this book published. Imprisonment doesn't remove a person's individual talents, but it very often suppresses them. A crucial part of our duty in caring for prisoners is to make sure that, so far as possible, the deprivation of liberty is the full extent of the punishment people suffer. So giving the opportunity for an individual prisoner to express his or her creativity is more than an optional extra; it is part of that duty of care.

For some people, this book represents what has made imprisonment bearable. I am proud both of the people whose work it contains and also of the staff and partners whose efforts have made it possible.

Peter Dawson
Governor

CONTENTS

I love you babe

I love you babe so very much
But while I'm here we hardly touch
We see each other every other week
I'm sad at night I cannot sleep
The visits are good we don't let go
Of each other we kiss so slow
It hurts us both when you have to go
One more year that's what we say
I worry and worry you'll go away
I know you won't, it's just this place
I wish now I could kiss your face
But soon I'll be free and we can do just that
I just can't wait till I can come back
xxxxxxxxx I Love You Babe xxxxxxxxx

Damian Hind

Untitled

Hear my voice
I am singing for you
Singing to you
Slip the locks and chains
From around your heart
Slip between those bars
Come into my arms

Cedric Poulina

Cedric Poulina - Untitled

Luke Gell - Untitled

The last lady

Listen, fair lady, why try
To lead me to a distant fantasy
Where life is filled with joy and family
Just to run when the going gets tough
Just to discard me like a bit of rough

That's not the way you deal with partnership
Next time be equipped to take a trip
Don't let yourself slip
Or the next partner might flip

So this is a lesson to be learned
Don't be a fool or next time it could well
Be you that gets burned!

Luke Gell

Hold onto your dreams

No matter what life brings
Onto your dreams
Just keep hold of them
Always cherish them
And treasure them like gold

For if you keep them in your heart
And nurture them each day
They will sprinkle you with magic
As you walk along life's ways

So keep this in your mind in
Everything you do
And very soon you will find
Those dreams will come true

Steven Brown

Robert G Clarke - Love Everything

Love everything

Love is what life is all about
We should grab it and make it count
Love is not just a human-to-human feeling
It's loving everything, living and being

We should love the air that we breathe
And not pollute the skies and the seas
We should love the water that we drink
But we waste it and we don't think

We should love the earth that we walk on
It gives us life and food also the clothes we put on
There are so many things we should love
But we choose not to see
Women having babies, born in a world of
Don't knows and maybes

What's deep down in the ocean
Living in peace and tranquility
While we're up above destroying our own humanity
We destroy life that gives us life
Tearing into the earth
Like cutting a cake with a knife

There's so many things we should be loving
Most of all we must stop the killing

Robert Clarke

Jez Court - Freedom

Stuck in a life

My head is in pieces but my mouth
Tells a different story
It lulls you into a false sense of security
That I will be alive the next time that you see me
I'm sorry, this is not how it was meant to be
But the solitude of death is a new
Lease of life for me
Don't grieve because death graced me early
Be happy that I'm in a place of fantasy
And not on these plains of tragedy

The life behind is now only a distant memory
But the love I kept will always be a friend to me
...I'm finally free

Luke Gell

Untitled

Wandering aimlessly through the park
Bored to tears, it's nearly dark
Listening to the trees rustling in the wind
It makes you wonder if they're trying to say something
Their roots buried deep in the ground
You think they want to break free and run around
I sit down and ponder, thinking of my life
It really is hard work, worries, and strife

Robert Clarke

David Faulkner - Untitled

Robert G Clarke - Let go

Let go

You start to wither like the leaves in autumn
You look frail like a rusty old pail
Fresh as a lemon has gone out of your complexion
Look in the mirror you dislike your reflection
You wish you could hide on the tallest mountain
Clouds below soft as a duck feather pillow
If only life was sweet as candy
You gave all your love
Never again trust me

Robert Clarke

Retrospect

He was looking back with regret
His form and art thumping through his head
Karma leaps, "Pat the funk"
Sings the hunk, Van-Heusen shirt
Hung with dirt
All for fun
Smiling high, radiant sun
Sunset's coming, looming dusk
Morning dawns, growing husky
Goodbye
Tragic....
Memory

Oscar Meki

Days out with dad

Days out with my Dad
Were times I seldom had
All my friends had holidays
And had a real good time
I had to say my Dad was away
I'd pretend that was fine

When he was out and home with us
It really was good fun
I really loved to be with him
From school to home I'd run
Every day he used to say
He would not go away

He loved us all, he cuddled us
He was always kissing Mum
Anytime it seemed to us
He would take us where he had to go

It never seemed to bother us
The pub, a fair, a show
My favourite was a football match
He'd make me feel so proud
He would sit me on his shoulders
So I could see above the crowd

The smells, the noise, the atmosphere
The swaying of the crowd
I swore that when I grew up
I'd never be like Dad
Well, I followed in his footsteps
My kids must think I'm sad

Glen Arnold

It's about time

I used to be a child
But I'm still in need
I'm growing up
In a world of greed
Part of a majority
That needs to be freed

This world is just madness
Bound by a lack of trust
And filled with sadness

It's like this because
People think the sky's the limit
They're fools
Blind and dim witted

It's about time people realised
That there's more beyond the skies
So gain some trust
Tell the truth
Don't tell lies
And live a life

Luke Gell

My son

I am proud I have a son
There's men out there who can't see their little one
Some leave because they just don't care
Some leave because it's hard to bear
Some leave because the relationship's broken down
Some leave because there's a new man in town
Some leave because they didn't want a child
Some leave because it wasn't their child
Some leave because they don't want responsibility
Some leave because they prefer all their money
Some leave because they're kids themselves
Some leave because they can't even look after themselves
I will not leave, my son means too much
Look deep in your heart and get in touch

Robert G Clarke

Robert G Clarke - My son

Four elements

Sunshine and sand
Lie in the palm of your hand
The powers that be
Which are invested in me
Shall be the bond
That breaks us free

I see the sea
All the waters that be
Ships and sail, glide and flutter
Giant waves crash and roar
On far-off desolate shores

I feel air blowing
Through my brazen hair
The air whistling
Of love everywhere
Like it has no cares

The fire burns, oh so bright
It lights hearth and lamp
All through the night
Your soul is all right
With pure delight
When the phoenix takes its flight

So blessed be
To all who see
The earth
The air
The fire
And the sea

Jason Page

Letter of sin

Yet another sentence
Done another crime
And gained penitence
What's the sense?

I dish out hurt like there's
No tomorrow
Why do I create so much sorrow?
Not just to family and friends
But also to people I will never know

I'm a foe of so many
Only because I take drugs and
Keep bad company
It once was funny
Now it's just the way
Do crime instead of scrimp and scrape
Some people would say I'm a fake

But this is real
You inconsiderate so-and-so's
Could never understand they way I feel
Because I'm trapped in a life where I have to steal
That's the only way to gain the next meal
And that's more real than you could imagine
So look at this paper and read this pen
Because I'm done

Luke Gell

Neil Jones - Untitled

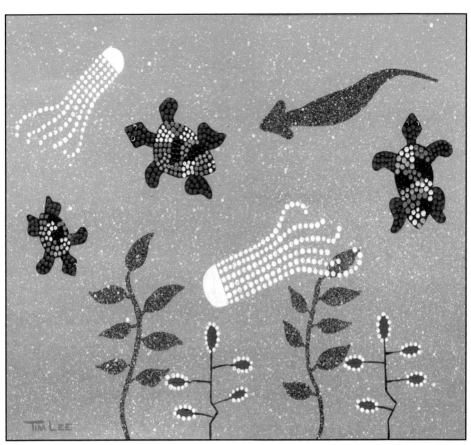

Tim Lee - Untitled

Sea side

The sea, as I slowly drive by
Come in to the shore on a wave so slow with the sun so high
Beaming down on passers by

The air of the sunny sea, the smell of sea salt brings back so
Many memories, of a place I used to be

The sand as I make my way down the beach, its warmness rolls
Beneath, sinking down as I come closer to the sea

The sea's salty air, flowing through the air
It's been so long, too long, to believe

The waves bounce off the beach
What a wonderful sight
Restored to me

It's time to take a dive
Time to feel the warmth
Of the
Ocean

The sea, see its distance as far as I can see
The saltiness, the warmth beneath my feet
The waves bounce off the beach
The warmth of the sea surrounds me

WOW, thought memories

Mac's

Lighter

It's about 3 inch long
Black with a silver top
A hole at the top
With a small wheel
And a flint

I got it from the shop
About 4 weeks ago
It didn't cost much
But in my time of need
Became very helpful
Almost like a best friend

I'm glad I got my light
Without it I'd be less independent
I always used to ask others
If I could borrow theirs
Which can be so disheartening

Sometimes it helps me when I stress
Light a roll-up and take away the craves
Saving me for selfless independence
Giving me the confidence
And ability to help others

But I sure do hope
Every smoker gets themselves a light
Sooner or later
I will start to have a new stress
If people keep asking me for a light

Mac's

Missing Sheldon

Sitting in your pram with a smile on your face
Different kinds of foods I'm trying to get you to taste
Looking around, my life seems such a waste
You should be able to play in a place more safe
Amazed proud and broke is how I feel
Your right in front of me but it still doesn't feel real
I've got to elevate myself and believe that I will
"Waa Waa" was the sound you would make when you cried
But it didn't bother me even in the middle of the night
I just wanted to make sure you was all right
Knock knock who's at the door
Always someone coming but the questions what for
Faintly hearing the answer from behind the door
Always in a fresh nappy and trackie pulling the hat off your head
The one picture that always stays in my head
In that room in that house on that street called friends
You showed me my heart wasn't as cold as I thought
Asking if I loved you reply to myself of course
But how can I be sure, love's something I've never felt before
Dipped eyebrows bottom lip tucked in
Screw face looking the same as mine
You brought a light and purpose to my life
But will you hate me because I was gone
Or can we just pick up where we left off

S M Johnson

Feel this

And though I hurt you in my thoughtless way
Last summer by omission and commission
I know what love was
Now it's thrown away

Sat alone, I rage at the incision
Self-inflicted, keeping us apart
When all I want or need is to be with you

I long to be imprisoned in your heart
To serve my time, erase my crime, be true

I hold a photo of you sleeping
Strands of loose hair fall across your face
Your hands are folded on your chest
Perhaps you dream of me
You often did

I listen, lean towards the glossy surface, place a kiss
On your pink lips
I dream you feel this

James Bull

Robert G Clarke - Street

Introducing mr H

You have heard about the Devil
And the world he lives in is hell
Well he's not as bad as me you know
There's a story I can tell
You see my name is heroin
Disgusting, dirty brown
Once you start to use me
Ill turn your life around
Ill control you cause without me
You'll have a sick, sad, scare
You'll lie, beg, steal, for me
Your life becomes a nightmare
Find yourself
Searching the streets for me
Hunting high and low
As your panic becomes unbearable
Your stomach will start to throw
It's all because of me you see
I'm often known as smack
Ill lead you to oblivion
And never bring you back
You'll destroy your friends and family
Ill turn your love to hate
A victim of my evilness
A sucker for my bait
I'm more evil than the devil
I'm wicked for your soul
I'm the plague in society
Ill even help to dig your hole
Yes it has been known for me to kill
But Id rather destroy your head
And leave you just to survive
As heroin's living dead
Heroin's living dead
Living dead
Dead

Slim

27

Transition

The dark has been my dreams of late
Any sense of which I can't relate
For the light has never been my fate
My destiny was crime
Life of prison I must state
That crime I was drawn to like proverbial bait
Of coke and crack my faithful mate
Without Id be in an off key state
Shot and stabbed and I feel great
Glamorising gangster I imitate
To self destruct I instigate
Within these lonely walls I suffocate
This winding road is far from straight
Oblivion and emptiness a heavy weight
These chains I can't unwind
Such a waste of life I contemplate
A change of life I must debate
This simple life I complicate
To normality I'm blind
Time to grow and appreciate
Talk the talk don't exaggerate
There's light at the end of the tunnel
It's not too late to change my mind

Mr R Wynter

Tyrone Mitchell - Untitled

Dee Roberts - Untitled

Handle with care

The old year crawled on hands and knees
Amazingly slow
His poor old beaten body
Carving deep bloody tracks
In the freezing snow

We kicked and laughed at his dying form
As he edged his way to the deep abyss
"Happy New Year" we shouted
Pushed him over
And midnight struck, we all kissed
Now he was gone

For twelve months we had treated him real bad
But here in his place was a
Bright new year, smiling
But for how long?
This sparkling, innocent, unsuspecting
Trusting little lad

Chris Christodoulides

Time

I've got time
Time on my hands
Time 2 blueprint my plans
Time 2 reflect
Time 2 c what's next
Time 2 regroup
Time 2 give old ways da boot
Time 2 plant seeds and reap fruit
Time 2 contemplate
Time 4 my mind 2 elevate
Time 2 try and get it straight
Time 2 meditate

Time 2 squat and bench
Time 2 get hench
Time 4 me 2 scream
Time 2 b quite
Time 2 dream
Time 2 control my out burst's and
refrain from being violent
Time 2 read books
Time 2 educate my chooks

Time 2 miss road
Time 4 summer 2 feel cold
Time 4 me 2 break da mould
Time 2 escape da sleeper hold
Time 2 wake up
Time 2 give a fuck
Time 4 me 2 stop cursing my luck
Time 2 b responsible
Time 2 start thinking logical
Time 2 b objective
Time 2 b progressive
Time 2 go forward and shine
Time 2 b 3 from doing time

Dee Roberts

Yelp!

I'm lost, someone
Please find me
This place can only be described
As larceny
I'm trapped, someone
Set me free
I'm bound by emotion and tragedy

Will I be free?
Will I be found?
Will I be left in this spot
To rot on the ground?

Here's a thought
Maybe no-one wants to find me
And I'm doomed to a life with no destiny
That's a sad state of affairs
Maybe it's best I leave
Because this is all to much
Stress for me

Luke Gell

Life in N15

Standing on the spot outside the local shop
Smoking, drinking waiting for school to finish
For the chicks to come out and to deal some business
Chatting to my mans with a blunt passing around
Talking to B about some shit that went down
My drinks done so I toss my glass to the ground
You can't hear it smash
Ask B if he wants something he replies "Na I'm safe"
So I go in the shop to buy a drink and still get one for my mate
As a car pulls up and the bass is loud
My man B moves away from the crowd
Jumps in the car but that aint nothing special
As he does another car pulls up next to
The one that he's in and lets off nuff shots
POP PA PA POP POP
Smoke rises from the wheels as it drives off
To kill B isn't what they wanted to do
But only he was going to have a funeral
Only two bottles smashing on the ground
Makes me realize the silence of the crowd

S M Johnson

David Clifton - Untitled

My DTTO
(Drugs Treatment and Testing Order)

Not too long ago
I breached my DTTO
I'm living on the streets
I can't get back on my feet
I am smoking crack
I am smoking brown

Damn this dirty old town
Wherever I go it's all around
It's on my streets and in my hood
Especially the bad neighbourhoods

The bad neighbourhood is where
I've been smoking crack
And doing ecstasy
I get so high it makes me queer
So I say, "Sod it, let's buy some more gear"

So I smoke some brown
To come down
I smoke some brown
I feel real nice
I feel so warm

Cam and collected tonight
Tonight is when the trouble began
I robbed a house
And some bloke's van

Now I'm back in court
Im bloody clucking
I go for bail
The judge said
"You must be joking,
Off the streets will stop you smoking"

So now I'm here
Back in jail
No hope, no mail
And no poxy bail

Jason Page

32

Wanted alive not dead

What lies in store in the year 2025
Will our precious planet still be alive?
Will man have made the forests burn
Beyond the point of no return

It's been a few years since the industrial revolution
And it hasn't taken long to cause global pollution
Will the ozone layer become depleted?
Allowing our planet to become overheated

How much ice on the poles will be there?
Not much hope for the polar bear
Will the fish in our rivers be under stocked?
Will the grasslands be bare, where sheep once flocked

What will become of many a coral reef?
By the hand of man ecological grief
Millions upon millions of spent nuclear rods
We must surely be in the lap of the gods

So what will become of our planet so dear?
With eyes closed shut it will become less clear
Perhaps it will become a great ball of dust
Ashes to ashes in ourselves we cannot trust

Ray Bradley

Greaves - Untitled

Night

In the dead of night
The wind, it sang
It bustled, it whistled
It broke down a branch
It blew over a thistle

The leaves, they danced
They twirled with delight
Like the flicker of a fire
In the heat of the night

The stars, they gleamed
They sparkled so bright
In the pale moonlight
Oh, what a lovely sight
In the dead of the night

So now, I bid you good night
Sleep tight

Jason Page

Mark Sale - Untitled

The weekend to end all weekends

After prison the voice of music in time
Can make hate change to love

Soon you're drunk and dancing in the street
You try shouting and feel love escape
From the prison within you

By chance a friendship forms at the pub
Two lovebirds kiss

A slow change of pain
You hear a familiar rhythm
A new life begins

Mark Sale

David Faulkner - Untitled

Night

It's getting harder to
Understand just what is happening to me
Is this the start, is this the end
What will it take to set me free?
I'm in a six-by-eight-foot box
Locked alone down in the hole
Strangled by the chains and the locks
And screaming deep down in my soul

Cedric Poulina

Untitled

I can't sit still for the tears in my eyes
Hoping on release I'm greeted with surprise
But still I know things aint gonna be great
Out of these gates to a wide world of hate

Dark clouds lie above me
There is silence in the skies
My vision is restricted, I have unseeing eyes
Darkness fills my thinking, my hearing is impaired
My feet have lost all spring, I walk among the scared

When first you're born your slapped to cry
To mothers womb you've kissed goodbye
Your day has come you learn to walk
And soon you find you too can talk
Your parents proud they walk with pride
Their precious child down by their side
Then its your teens, its time to leave
To see what you too can achieve
But the hands of time, they move so fast
Because as you blink your life has past

Plenty of ambitions but no strength to reach em
If I see my girls, so much I wanna teach em
Like stay away from plastic bad boys and con men
Or end up in jail where they'll meet them
Prison is a place where they enforce their rules
Prison is a place where you find your balls
Prison has ups, prison has downs
Prison has smiles, but mostly frowns
Prison has a king the governor wears the crown
Prison has a queen who is never around
Prison has one aim, to deprive you of time
Prisons are designed to make you think of your crime

Hubbard

Me

I'm made of glass
Not the fragile kind
Not the eggshell thinness
Of a light bulb
Waiting for a heavy hand
Or barefoot stamp to
Shatter it.

What I feel is heavy
The heft of the bottom of
A bottle made of thick
Green glass
That catches light and
Holds it in itself
Reflecting inward

I am unreactive.

My only action is a
Millennial slump.
I'm not quite solid,
Imperceptibly flowing in a
Glacial spread.
I count in geological units
The time until I sleep
It tires me.
What's a day or night when
Every hour's like this?

Break me
Throw me in the sea to
Scour me,
Scrub away the edges so I
Never hurt again

James Bull

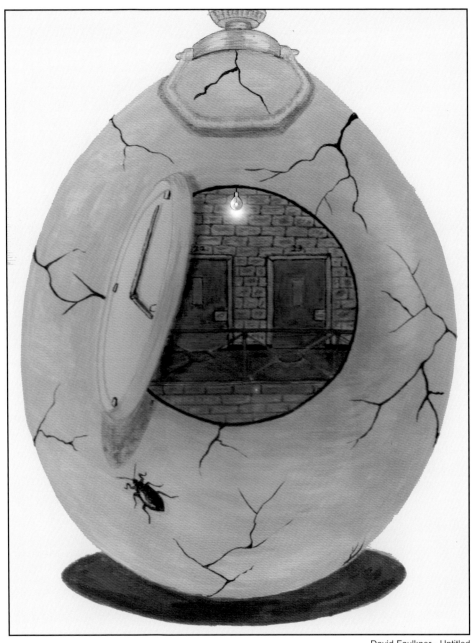

David Faulkner - Untitled

Cedric Poulina - Untitled

Tainted

She always wanted a tattoo
Something to reflect
Her wildflower image

Her boyfriend accompanied
Her
She requested
He have one too

Not only that
But
Her name
On his chest

You first
She said
This day will symbolise
Our affection
She said

He did
And she replied
Mine forever

Dee Roberts

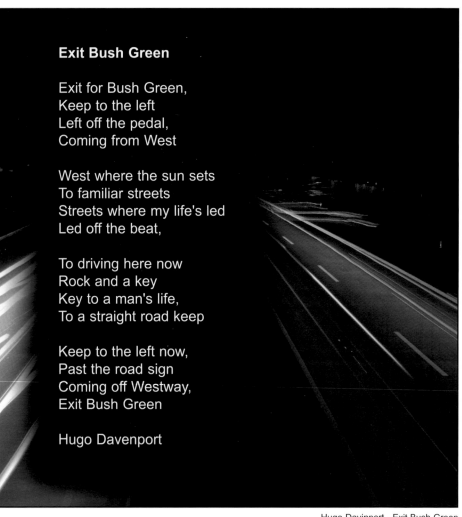

Exit Bush Green

Exit for Bush Green,
Keep to the left
Left off the pedal,
Coming from West

West where the sun sets
To familiar streets
Streets where my life's led
Led off the beat,

To driving here now
Rock and a key
Key to a man's life,
To a straight road keep

Keep to the left now,
Past the road sign
Coming off Westway,
Exit Bush Green

Hugo Davenport

Hugo Davinport - Exit Bush Green

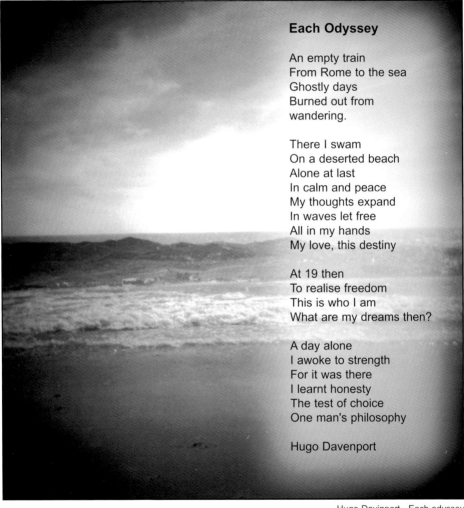

Each Odyssey

An empty train
From Rome to the sea
Ghostly days
Burned out from
wandering.

There I swam
On a deserted beach
Alone at last
In calm and peace
My thoughts expand
In waves let free
All in my hands
My love, this destiny

At 19 then
To realise freedom
This is who I am
What are my dreams then?

A day alone
I awoke to strength
For it was there
I learnt honesty
The test of choice
One man's philosophy

Hugo Davenport

Hugo Davinport - Each odyssey

David Clifton - Untitled

Tooting summers

Come, let us roam the night together
If we leave now, we will avoid the trouble

Summer night's empty cans
Pretty girls in short skirts
With big crack addicts

We live to survive, but
To survive is never enough.

Come, let us roam the night together

Steven Valentine

Share the sky

We share the moon, you and I
We share this red stained sky
Silence divides, our eyes shan't meet
Through wire and stone
No hands can reach

So as seasons sink behind the walls
Of you I dream, let dead leaves fall
Your carefree beauty haunts my mind
No greater prize could life define

To meet your eyes, to feel your touch
To this place now, this asks too much;
Yes we share the dawn
The breeze, the dusk,
Held apart in all but love.

Hugo Davenport

Hugo Davinport - Share the sky

My Guiding Star

My guiding star
That's what you are
You're always near
You're never far
You gave me love
When I was down
You're the only one
Who was around
My guiding star

David Jones

Untitled

I stand before you
And I smile
You smile back
And I notice
How your eyes seem to sparkle
With loves sincere affection

Caswell Holness

Damian Hind - Untitled

What if

What if I was not me but I was you
What if you was not you but you was me
What if you had to live in the same place as me
And made the same mistakes as me
What if you were living in constant hell
What if you got arrested and got no bail
What if after reading this you were going back to my cell
What if

S M Johnson

Moving

Her wide tyres
Clinging and pinning herself to the road
Agile and fast like a puma
Yet stately,
Regal like a beast

While outside cold-looking
All business no mess
Inside lies warm comfort
A pocket to rest

Black with tints, immaculate
Driving her gives me a lift
When life was too heavy
To the motorways I'd take

Thinking only of the two lines
My lane, nothing else
The panels worked with me
She'd hide what I'd give

At raves I slept
Drunk in her seats
Now she's still waiting
To take to the streets

Hugo Davenport

The Book

Oh to lose myself within a book
But Iv only got a bible, shall I take a look?
From Genesis to revelations, Ill read it through
And discover the love given to you
I'm not a Christian; The books not mine
Should I read on, or stand and decline?

Iv read about mans first mortal sin
Why Adam and Eve let the Devil in
When Lucifer, disguised, with serpents tongue
Breathed the lie into human lung
And how God, intensified with rage
Recorded their sin on a pristine page

But I'm not a Christian, as I said before
And to read this book could be a chore
Alas, to my sorrow and lasting shame
I found that God has got a name
"Emmanuel", the old prophets cried
Telling of his son and how he died

My life could change if I would but see
Just how this book relates to me
Will I ever find heaven on this earth?
Or remain condemned to my fiery berth
Oh no! Not me, I had a look
Now I know why I read that book

Maybe my days of sin can end
I read that book, and found a friend

Grant D

Prison Window

Sitting down looking through my prison window
Thinking about what I would be doing other than smoking indo
Feeding the pigeons or should I say birds
Watching them shut down Rasta road where I use to get my herbs
This is my 3rd time in this shit man when would I learn
Rizzla still rolling that bitch Virginia now that's there's me burn
Got youths out on road that should be my main concern
Sitting on a "L" plate feeling fucked even though parole in 2008
Still stuck between thoughts should I work or educate
Trying to narrow down my circle from the clowns who are fake
But everywhere I turn like screws there everywhere you go
Pulling hard on my burn looking thru my window wishing it was
krow

Michael Yankee Palmer

49

Rash - Untitled

We Have No

We have no name to give our dreams
We have no destination to forget our past
We have no reflection to see ourselves in dreams
We have no-body to compare ourselves
We have nothing to fear alone in these dreams

Caswell Holness

Tim Lee - Untitled

Various Thoughts!

I see a beautiful sky in my sight
The golden sunrays appear through the clouds
Inspiring my life
But it still seems im stuck in a fight
Struggling to keep away from carrying a gun or a knife
The white bars keep me depressed in my room
But I know the metal doors will reopen my life soon
Away from stress, seeing my daughters face
Will fill me with bloom
Joy, happiness, love and peace from evil im immune
For now I gaze at the world's creation
Reciting ones name because Ive found realisation
His name has guided me and made me patient
Reading his book shows me pictures
And I stare in imagination
This is the room where I experience my life dreams
One cuts his arm and the other one screams
What do I learn from this, what does this mean?
This is a lesson everyday I gain knowledge
I sit uncomfortably
Thoughts about my past leave cold my porridge
I can't wait to eat some Kentucky fried chicken
But my family and my daughter
Is the one im really missing

Pahul "Illusion" Sandhu

R J McDowell - Untitled

From me to you

My grandmother enjoyed growing vegetables and crops on the farm
You can almost see the labour by looking through her hands
Transforming from my grandmother to my mum
She had an onerous task in keeping me in line
The chase! The catch!
The slaps! The smack!
Everything is starting to make sense now
It was all part of the process of maturing me into a man

I feel helpless and desolate now that she is aging old
Wishing I could inject some life into her decaying bones
I can't help reminiscing about the time she used to wipe the bogey from my nose
Now I can only worry for her when the weather starts to snow
Hoping that her immune system would be able to cope
During my adolescence she made sure that there was always vitamins in my bowl
Whether the weather was stormy cloudy or cold
She was adamant that there would be food to reap from the soil

My grandmother's trade marks were indigenous from within
The way she used to cut her eyes and kiss her teeth
It was like a direct warning aimed at me
Almost to say
"Do that again and you will get a smack in the face"
I will always remember my grandmother's ways
Especially when I am enduring one of those dreadful days
Or when I am in the kitchen by the racketeering of the pots, pans and plates

I remember how we used to sit in the night around the burning fire
The silhouette in her face illuminated so much desire
My grandmother she wasn't much of a dresser
She kept it together
By simply modelling her traditional attire
Now that I am taller and wiser
There is one question I have yet to ask her
Did she ever get tired from working hard like a robot farmer?
Suddenly I arrive at a sensible answer
Working hard was part of her calibre
Part of her dynamic character

Emmanuel Imagemite

Emmanuel Imagemite - From me to you

Emmanuel Imagemite - Too much to go through

Too much to go through

Before you choose to fall in love
Be prepared to hurt
Before you prepare to hurt
Be ready to cry
Before you proceed to cry
Buy some tissues to dry your eyes
Before you purchase some tissues
Deal with your issue
Before you battle with your issue
Be careful who you choose
Before you decide to choose
Think everything through
Even from the colour of their hair
To the size of their shoes
Before you judge by the size of their shoes
Ask yourself if you are prepared to be true
Because when you fall in love
You become a fool

Emmanuel Imagemite

Desperately seeking hope

We hold on to hope
Like the night holds on to tomorrow
For if there were no nights
There would be no tomorrow
The morning awakens the sorrow
The beginning of the uphill struggle
As we climb up the hill
We encounter so many battles
The path becomes short and narrow
Staying appeased at times becomes a mission impossible

But with hope we are able to cope
In hope there is misery
In hope there is tragedy
In hope there are promises
In hope there are fantasies
Hope is a lethal positivism
It has no affinity with reality
But as faithful human beings
We are willing to believe in the possibilities
But as long as there is a view through the window
And as long as there is always tomorrow
There will always be hope

Emmanuel Imagemite

Untitled

I am here, HMP Highdown
Serving my sentence for the crown
All I do is think of you
So when I get out were still true

Iv had enough of the crime
Now I'm inside I'm getting the sign
So don't be a mug and get in line

So all these words I write to you
Are so very much so true
And all Iv done is break your heart
To say the least it wasn't smart

I regret the things Iv done
Believe me baby there is more than one

If I could change the time to nil
I promise I wouldn't lie cheat or steal

So all my heart I send to you
Make sure you love it like I love you

Dodger

Cedric Poulina - Untitled